You, Me, and Her

You, Me, and Her

Cover design by Melissa Freitas

Book Copyright ©2018 Tylyn Taylor

All Rights Reserved

This book or any portion thereof may not be reproduced or used in any manner whatsoever without the express written permission of the author except for the brief quotations in a book review.

Preface

I know what it feels like to wish your life away. To beg the sun to set on you, and the moon to say it's final goodbye. I know what it's like to love someone so completely that you take their burdens and carry them on your back, so that they can be free. And I know what it's like to have that person beat those burdens into your flesh. And you forgive, and you forgive, and you forgive again, all the while slowly losing yourself.

This book started out as a collection of journal entries and poems written over the course of two years, during a relationship that proved both emotionally and physically abusive. It was the sole outlet that would eventually save my life. As a woman I take pride in my independence, strength, intelligence, and bravery. I never imagined someone would have the power to take that from me. But love is a funny thing, and if I am anything, it's love in all its forms. I broke my heart open to try and save someone else and it almost destroyed me, yet despite everything, I found beauty in hope. Who I wanted to be was still living inside of me, she just had to claw her way out.

I took the time to heal, learn, and to fight like hell to be the woman I have always dreamed of being. The road is long and hard, and some days are worse than others, but everything in my future is incomparable to what lays dead in my past.

I wrote this book so that other women would know that they are never truly alone—that they are still worthy. That they, too, are love. It may feel like you are never going to get out of these situations alive, spiritually or physically, but you can. You can leave, you can survive, and you can still be everything you've ever wanted to be. And you will love again. I want this book to be a manifestation of that for every pair of hands that hold onto it.

Feral

I get that I'm not the girl

With the word sweetheart draped across her neck

My mouth paints words like graffiti

With fuck in black ink

And I don't use my big toothy smile

To plaster "I'm okay" on my face

Because I'm not

And my teeth are cracked and chipped

Like the heart on my sleeve

They deem my journeys wild

A feral energy of a woman

Exuding an unruly aura

As I move with the tides

Unpredictable at best

Though I've been called far worse

But this isn't their story to tell

Or their title to give

It's mine.

Demand Your Experience

I wish I had realized a long time ago that I had this voice inside of me that was meant to be shared.

This reckless, fearless, sound that vibrates on a higher frequency.

We all have it. Etched inside each of us is our purpose. What we are meant to radiate out into the world. And the problem is, so few of us bring forth that power. We don't demand what is inherently ours until we are forced to.

Until it is challenged out of us.

We carry the weight of trepidation, and we blame it on lack of means, or the practicality of life. But it is what we deserve. We deserve to share. To be seen. To be valued and heard. Don't get in your own way of that.

Because I wish I wouldn't have spoken in hushed tones. Or been what I thought everyone else wanted me to be.

I starved myself that right of life. I looked outward for purpose, when I always should have been looking in. Because like the cypress tree my roots run deep, begging to be seen above ground.

And I shouldn't have seen my kindness as a liability. Because you can be dangerous and still sweet all in one. In fact, that is the most lethal combination of woman there is. You deserve to stand your ground and stretch out your limbs. This is your space. This is your experience. I know the

pain doesn't seem worth it at the time. That coming un-tethered from the monster pinning us down will exhaust our spirit. And it might. But monsters are meant for fairytales, and you were meant for epics.

You will survive. And your light will radiate from the pain. Your experiences will cultivate the true self. So, don't cut yourself down to be used for other people. Feed the roots. Let yourself bloom in front of the world. And do it for you. Not for the monster you buried, or the you, you think looks good on paper.

You do it for your conscious self. And you grow. And your growth carries on for hundreds of years. You are strength. Your frequency is picked up.

And the hope is it vibrates on the wavelength of those who need it. That they recognize you're light because they've seen it in themselves. When they are alone and shed their skin and are in that moment of sincere identity. They recognize that extension of true self.

Then they demand it. They take up space. They sow the land. They do the work, and they find their voice.

There is a combination in all of us meant to be seen, if we are willing. So, accept the challenge.

It's yours to face.

Honey

All I want is a love that fills my mouth with honey

That pours sweet nothings from my lips

Someone who permeates my soul with adventure

And catches my tears in the palms of their hands

Sticky and sweet

Soft

While loving hard.

Worth

You aren't one wave

You're the whole fucking ocean.

Butterflies

I knew it would end eventually

But I clung to your promises

The way your eyes lit up when you talked about the future

Our future

But we never really had a chance, did we?

Because your past showed up on your face

Before I even had a chance to hold your hand

And I thought if I just helped carry the weight

We could make it

But the heavy lifting wasn't meant for my shoulders

And you can't take other people's burdens

And turn them into butterflies.

Standards

I am a woman who chooses not to rush. I take my heart seriously and I love fiercely, but I refuse to settle. I refuse to apologize for refraining when something doesn't feel right. I know exactly what I want out of this life, and I fight for it every day. So why wouldn't I hold the same standards when choosing a partner?

I am not talking about building walls, or holding reservations, by all means dive right in when you feel connection with someone. Those are some of the most beautiful moments we experience with people; rolling around in the sheets, talking about everything and nothing at the same time. Venting out our hopes and dreams to another set of sultry eyes. Vulnerability is not a fear of mine. Cracking my heart wide open is something I do every day. But connections fade, no matter how much we try and sustain them. If you are all in and the other person isn't, then they are not worth your fight. If they find your willingness for love, and life, and wanting to share moments with them intimidating, or they don't feel the same, then your energy serves no purpose there.

You deserve the stars.

And in no world is loving with the entirety of your being a liability to your character. Having the grace to know when it's time to let go is one of the hardest struggles we will ever have in life. But settling for a love that doesn't scale mountains is worse. Because if it isn't a "hell yes, I'm all in," from the other person, then it should be a "fuck no" from you. You were not born to chase. You were not put on this earth to convince another heart to beat for you.

You are here to raise hell. We get one shot at this thing, and I want to look back on a life filled with an epic love story, even if that means years of edits and revisions until my story comes along and prints itself permanently on my pages.

So, don't rush.

Take your time. Love hard. Never apologize for having that fire inside of you for more. Because someday, someone is going to light that fire, and honey fireworks will light up your world.

Hope

The blood from my heart is on your hands again

And I said I didn't want these problems

But I left my door unlocked for you to walk through

And I let your voice put me to bed

Then you were gone the next morning

And all of my wounds were split open

Leaving me to revel in the chaos once again

I used to think a life without you was death

But this time I'm able to stitch myself up

With crooked loose threads

That may come unraveled again

But each time you walk away I'm stronger

More resilient

And I'm sure another woman was silently screaming your name

As you were wrapped up in me

I hope she finds the strength that I never could

Or knows herself more than I ever have

And the thing that propels me forward

Is that I know someday I'll lock the door

You, Me, and Her

Your knocks will fall silent to my ears

And I won't be the high that cures your narcissism for the night ever again

Because I am no longer afraid

Losing you for good isn't my biggest fear anymore

It's my only hope.

Fire

I've met too many men lately

Who run from the fire in my eyes

Instead of reveling in it.

Made to Love

When you experience a love that seems like it was meant to be, it feels as if it was written in the stars. Formed in the cosmos, and sent to this galaxy, thick with moon dust and enchantment. Just waiting to set fire to two souls, using the Earth's magnetic pull to collide two separate worlds.

And that's what we had.

A fate that brought two people together on a crowded beach in the tropics. Falling for each other the moment honey spilled from their lips, in the form of a name.

You had a smile that rivaled the Hawaii sun, and jet-black curls that bounced right above dark brown eyes. I had never seen another human being so beautiful. And I never felt more alive, than when my legs were tangled up in yours, on soft white sand, under a Kailua moon.

And the island played her part in it all. Using her salty air, and blue waters to put us in a trance.

Getting lost in her jungle and stealing kisses deep in her green mountains.

I can still hear your laugh; through sips of beer, over sticky rice and mangoes. And I could have watched you talk with your hands for the rest of my life.

But not even an endless summer can last forever. And the Midwest was pulling me back.

An ocean stood between us, but I would have scaled mountains just to touch your hand. Because I craved your presence, in a way only a soul mate can when it's been displaced from its counterpart.

But the history you carried with you was heavy, and it disrupted our planets alignment. You didn't see yourself the way my green eyes did. So you cracked me wide open, and carved the word broken into my chest.

Venom dripped from your tongue over empty beer cans, and you no longer used your hands for just speaking.

And I even loved you then, when your shame showed up in black and blue on my arms.

And your presence was never guaranteed.

Now, you seem so far away. And that's the problem with a destiny forged in the stars. It burns out. Shooting through the night sky, hot and fast, and fizzling out beyond the eyes reach.

And sometimes I feel you in my chest. That maybe we still dream the same dreams.

My heart still beats for you, in some ways it always will, even when I beg it to stop.

But I hope someday you are able to love yourself the way I always have, because life is so short. And we will never make it out alive.

And you may not be my one and only, or my forever.

But that's okay. Because I've learned without you, I can be the love of my life.

I'll be the story the sun whispers to the moon.

And I'll find strength in taking the pieces you broke a part in me,

And build my own masterpiece.

Mom

I wish I could go back and hold my mother's hand

When she was eighteen and watched her father take his last breath

I would wipe away her tears and tell her it isn't her job to carry the weight of the world

Or of her family

I would tell her that it is okay to say no

That she should go now

That she should run

Her potential holds no bounds

And a heart likes hers was meant to hold thousands

A magnetic smile is hard to come by

And hers could pull metal from the earth

I would tell her that her worth doesn't come from the men who love her

Or the number of children who have lived in her womb

I wish she could see herself the way everyone else does

Now, her hands are hard from protecting five children

And her embrace is soft and warm

Her heart is divided among everyone who needs her

Leaving no fraction meant for herself

And I wonder what she wonders about

If she thinks about that eighteen-year-old girl like I do

And I hope she finds her again

And I get to meet her

Because she deserves a life filled with bliss

And it's time she gave that to herself

I Want Me

I was 22 when I fell in love with a man on a beach in the tropics. To admit that it was love at first sight would be admitting that my reality was a cliché, yet it was.

I can still feel the hot sand competing with my face that day as it flushed at the site of you.

A mountain of a man.

Tall and strong, contagious. Laughter that swept me up and made me lose all sense of self. If love is blind, I was deaf and mute.

You always kept your eyes covered. As if hiding behind ray-bans could hide the fact that you had no integrity.

Today, I'm 24 and your broken promises are still written on my walls.

And the bed we shared has stayed empty, because I can't stand to sleep where you once did.

I should have left when you finally showed your eyes.

When the smell of her breath was still on your lips, as you called to tell me "I love you."

And I should have left when the pain you inflicted on me came with your hands around my neck.

But I didn't.

I regret that.

Now, everyone says you weren't worth the trouble. That I will find someone that deserves all of this love I still have left inside of me.

And even though they are right, I don't want that.

I don't want a new version of you with a bag of their own tricks.

I want to love me.

The me that existed before you.

The me who didn't cry a little when she laughed, because happiness was always fleeting with you.

Me, who never doubted or wondered about my own worth, because you always made me feel less than.

I want the me that fought back.

The one that never even tripped over a man who couldn't handle a strong woman.

I deserve all of the love I have left inside of me. You didn't use me up.

Because this right now, my reality, is not a cliché.

I'll leave that up to you.

My Apology

Pardon me if you don't understand me

If my emotion for life is too big and swallows you whole

If my refusal to live a life I don't find extraordinary fills you with apprehension

Or makes you feel uneasy

If my inclination to love scares you off

Because I refuse to pull back even when I'm broken

And I'm sorry if you got washed away in my tide

As the moon was pulling me in different directions

And I acknowledge that maybe you think I am silly

That my day dreams were meant for shooting stars

But I'd rather chase this wonder for the rest of my life

Than lay back and watch it all go by

Because I am a silly woman most days

And a wild woman every night

And you may say I'm righteous

And that I feel too much

That's fine

You, Me, and Her

I'm sorry if you were under the assumption that I was here to please you

But I do not belong to you

You are not entitled to me or my passion

So my condolences if the fire that drips from my tongue turns you off

Because fuck is a four-letter word

And so is love

And there's a fine line

So, don't mistake my smile as a liability

Or my light as an invitation

And if you're going to run with me

You better shoot magic from the hip

Because I can run all by myself, baby

Honestly, I prefer it.

Unlearning

You know when you start to wonder what they wonder about?

That's how I knew.

Knew I wanted it to be real.

So naturally I had to destroy any chance of it being more meaningful than late nights wrapped up in each other's legs.

Because my history forces me to create a problem before they see the real problem—me.

And this stems from something bigger than having my guard up.

My past left third degree burns on my heart that I haven't taken the time to heal yet, and the ashes show up on men who have nothing to do with it. Thick and black, smudging any redeeming quality I may have conjured up with them the night before.

And the ironic thing is, I know this is what I do. I hurt men before they have a chance to find out anything real about me. I place blame on a kind face and strong hands that don't deserve it.

   I can destroy mutual respect with one text message.

I give someone I'm falling for a reason to want absolutely nothing to do with me.

And I know it isn't right, but I am messy at my core. It's all twisted up and broken. Nothing makes sense and anxiety fills the spaces that were once open to love.

And maybe I'm afraid they'll see those messy parts and run, so I cause chaos that forces them to run first. But I still recognize the parts of me that were once easy to hold. I still try and make a home in my arms for men who want to be there. And we can't expect an "I'm sorry, I'll do better" to wipe away the "fuck you" we hurled at someone hours before.

But I am working on change.

And it may not always look like it, because I'm stuck in this cycle of wanting someone to stay, but forcing them to go.

The problem is I don't know how to love anymore.

I don't know how to open my heart up to another person properly, because I don't want to.

I am scared.

Scared to let go, scared of change, scared to see if my heart can handle another blow. I know I'm not alone in this.

And it's the fear that closes us off in these situations. I recognize that. We have to sit with this fear and challenge it. Let it pull the growth from within us.

We have to do it.

Because we will never find peace in the arms of another. Even if they have a grin that makes your knees weak, and a voice that makes your heart race.

It has to start with you.

No Longer

No longer

Will I share my voice

My bed

My body

With men who only live

For the fleeting

Moments

I came to collect

Mine

My time

Is too valuable

To be wasted

On a black towel

In the corner

Of your bedroom.

Spoon Rings

I met a man

Who whispered he was in love with the flecks of gold in my green eyes

A man who held my neck in his hands

As he devoured my body whole

My fingernails digging deep into the flesh of his back

On top of lavender scented sheets

And when we made each other laugh

A sly smile would dance over his lips

A small gap peeking through his two front teeth

An imperfection that made my knees weak

And when I tried to learn what lived in his chest

He'd kiss every inch of my face

Laughing without ever revealing

Because avoidance was his weapon of choice

And silence filled the space between us
Whenever I got too close to finding out.

You, Me, and Her

I met a man

But I never actually knew him

Even though I could tell you what he tasted like

And how his hands felt cupping my face

We both hold intimate pieces of each other

And I don't even know his middle name

He decided I wasn't worth anything more

Than 2am on a Tuesday night

And my 25th year started out with my legs tangled in his

But I hope I forget about his existence entirely

That my wonder dissolves into a slight memory

Of just another man who fought the fire in my eyes

With fear

Because my worth can't be calculated by a man

Who witnesses my passion

And deems my love unsafe

A man afraid to dive below the surface

Will never connect with me on a cosmic level

But I do think it's silly

That a woman like me

Put so much weight into someone like him

Because I'm not afraid to let my boldness rule

Or tell another person how they make my heart beat

Faster

You will know exactly how I feel

The moment we touch hands

And authenticity wasn't even in his vocabulary

I met a man

but I wouldn't categorize him as one.

The Sea

I always feel sad at first. I go licking the wounds my ego took when someone doesn't want to make plans with me anymore, or they quit texting back.

I can't help but think of all the work I do, the manifestation that has helped me in most aspects of my life — except for this.

I put the good energy out, in hopes of it to return. I yell up at the sky, shaking my fists.

"Universe show me a man with a heart as big as the ocean."

And she will give me men, with auras of a sunset sky. And I usually connect quick.

Maybe it's my willingness to love. Or my faith in shared laughter.

I like to pull the best parts of a person out of their third eye and dance with them.

So, I go and I paint their colors in my room. And we lay tipsy on the hardwood floor, taking small sips of red wine. Pressing our palms together, until we feel each other's heart race in our own wrists.

We spend the night together, exchanging stories under cotton sheets. Only breaking eye contact for iced-coffee and condom runs.

But the brightness of it always fades. The paint begins to chip, and all I'm left with is empty spaces, and an unkempt bed, with water rings that stain my night stand.

And these men she provided for me, they stop being funny. Their once sweet smile seems sinister and their hands begin to look small. Then they start to forget dates and don't honor your time. Because theirs means more to them than yours ever will.

And showing up is only for real men.

But they didn't see you anyway. I mean *really* see you. And people will say you shared your bed too soon, that physical connection should be suppressed until date five. As if sex is the only thing you have to offer, as if it's the best thing.

"Why would they buy the cow, if they can get the milk for free?"

Fuck your milk and your cow. I'm a woman. And I'm sexual and strong, while still being soft and intelligent. But these partners who don't respect us make us feel less than.

You, Me, and Her

And you'll begin to wonder;

Am I enough?

Am I too much?

What do I fix?

You realize fate is testing you, on these things the partner designed for you will already know;

That you are enough.

You can never be too much.

Your beauty is embedded in the cracks.

And when you finally meet him, his hands will be able to hold a woman like you. Because his heart beat is in sync with your crashing waves.

He won't dismiss your showing up as a character flaw, because he will have already been waiting for you, with an embrace as big as the sea.

Falling in Love

She felt the way the stars must

As they dance around the moon.

Norma Jane

Some men's entire lives are shaped by their father.

A chip off the old block.

Formed with car grease, and an old baseball mitt.

That is not the case of my father.

Who entered this world as his family's sixth man.

Looking up at four older sisters, and a distant brother.

All of them held together by a woman that I believe could literally move mountains.

A woman way ahead of her time.

Who ran a kitchen in an old bowling alley,

So she could feed six growing humans,

Because her husband couldn't put down the drink.

And his burden was so heavy it broke him.

But she carried it with ease,

Because you can't break a woman like this.

And she smoked cigarettes with her favorite celebrities.

This is a woman who asked Pete Rose if she could touch his thigh.

And of course, he let her.

She never takes shit from anyone.

Not even from the man who gave her children their last name.

She thought about letting it all burn down once, the house with him in it.

While a lit cigarette sat between his lips as he slept off a hangover

But her heart is as big as she is stubborn.

And she turned around and walked back in, before the flame could catch their sheets.

And she will laugh big laughs with you and call you simple.

When she's pissed her eye brow shoots up to her hairline.

I swear to God it could still make grown men shake.

She helped raise all of her children's children.

And even their children.

Whose ages range from forty-three to seven.

She fed us sweetened coffee, and macaroni without any cheese.

We liked it best that way.

And she'd tell us stories about her family,

About a father who she barely knew.

And she's never told me much about her own mother

But I guarantee you she was tough as hell.

Because only a woman could grow another person like a cypress tree.

And she learned it from somewhere.

Because she cultivated 6 incredible human beings,

And buried one of them too soon.

He was a rock star.

So in the worst way it makes sense that he left us early.

The best ones always do.

Imagine carrying a pain like that around with you every day,

And still being soft enough to hold everyone in your arms.

Without her, people wouldn't stop me in coffee shops and know my last name,

Because they think I look like all of her daughters.

And I wouldn't have my father's face.

And I wouldn't be me.

Because you see, my father's entire life has been molded by women.

And he works on cars for a living,

And was one hell of a baseball player.

But I guarantee you he would tell you all about his mother,

Before he even mentioned his father.

Because there's something to be said about sturdy women, who grow great men.

Men who know how to raise three little girls.

With all of the love and compassion in the world.

Men who have learned to be a great father,

Because of their mother.

Tom-boy Dreams

I wish I would have grown up in a world where being beautiful wasn't the most sumptuous thing I could be. That the words I dropped from my mouth held more weight than the color of my hair.

Or the measurement of my waist. And I wish I hadn't spent so much time hating the traits that were deemed my flaws; Loathing the fact that I never had huge tits, or that I felt more like myself with a basketball in my hand than a makeup brush.

And I hate that I grew up being told what women could and couldn't be. That dark eye liner meant you were easy, but not enough labeled you plain.

That I could make a man genuinely laugh until he was blue in the face, and in his next breath he'd remind me that women are just simply, not funny.

And it makes my skin crawl recalling high school math class, listening to girls talk in baby voices and pretending that they understood nothing, because being dumb meant being cute.

Now, I can't help but wonder how many of us knobby kneed, plaid skirt wearing girls would have made a difference if we didn't try so hard to prove that our brains were the least attractive parts about us.

As an adult, I've begun to shed the repression that once covered my epidermis. I've locked eyes with the power that lives in my own throat.

And still, I've had men try to bully it out of me, because they didn't like the sound of my melody.

And women have rolled their eyes at me and whispered that I wasn't a lady.

I've been too much.

Not enough.

I've been called every name in the book…and then some.

And I don't have regret, but if I could have just strung these words together when I was seventeen,

like I can now, and screamed them at the top of my lungs;

I don't give a fuck.

Because I don't need to be anything for anyone, except myself. And I can't stop thinking about the skinny thirteen-year-old little girl I was, wearing basketball shorts, and a tangled pony tail on top of my head.

And I hurt for her.

Because I wish someone would have told her that it's okay not to fit in, to feel, and be different. That other people's judgments have nothing to do with her, and everything to do with them.

That the reflection in the mirror didn't mean anything compared to the strength coursing through her veins, and the ideas she had dancing around in her head.

My hope is that this world continues to change. That my three nieces grow up knowing that they can be anything they want to be.

And they can do it with a full face of makeup on or barefoot with dirty hands.

That women continue to make noise.

To be a force.

That we stomp out each other's doubts with muddy combat boots, or new red bottoms. That no one can tell us what we can or can't be, because together we are everything.

That is the world I want to continue living in.

That is the world I will fight for.

Young Love

The moon chased the tail lights in your old Toyota

And we never beat my curfew home

When love was long driveways and wearing your sweatshirt

After football games on Friday night

Simple

Back then I could have sworn it would last forever

But time changed my mind

And we traded each other in for freedom

Now you'd be a stranger

And me just another girl

But I loved you the way one does

When you're seventeen and your heart has never been cracked.

I've Yet to Meet a Lover

I have yet to encounter a lover

Who can ignite the embers in my soul

A man eager to explore the galaxy that encompasses my body

Does not seem to live in this realm

I've been slapped with the title intimidating

Because I only laugh

When something is actually funny

And the soles of my feet are tired of searching

I've got better stories to cultivate

So I let them exist here

For a night or maybe two

And little boys run off

After they've felt the flesh of my inner thighs

But I keep their secrets with me here

How their hands are not big enough

To hold the heart of a woman

With the power of the ocean.

Unsafe

I loved him the way you can only love a person once

Where you claw at each other's wounds

Letting the open flesh bleed out

And you sew each other up

Just to make love over broken glass on the floor

Tweaking until you get the next fix

Purpose

Bleeding from one another's ribcage.

Eggshells

My heart lays cracked

Like eggshells on the counter

And I still feel your rage inside of me

Flirting with the veins pulsing through my wrists

Today your home smells of a different ocean than mine

But I wonder if you'll ever leave me

Because when I judge myself I'm looking through your dark eyes

And it's your hands on my body

And your voice seeps through the empty corners of my mind

But I still love you

And that makes me hate myself.

Do Not Reply

I asked you not to contact me

For my own health

But you can't help yourself

You feed on getting a reaction out of me

Urging me to hit reply

And let the poison spew from my cheeks

The toxicity fills you up

Keeping you tethered to me

You feel relevant

But my life means more than any hate either of us could call on

And this is a narrative I no longer wish to write

Because our entire relationship was an extravagant pity party

That was thrown for you

Even though I was the one with ice packs on my eyes

And your words once fought your battles

When your fists weren't leaving bruises on my flesh

But now they have fallen silent

You, Me, and Her

You take up no space here

And the reply button is always tempting

Begging me to remind you how volatile you really are

Because I remember a time you burned the word worthless into my chest

And your name almost danced across my wrists in red

Leaving anxiety and shame to fill the empty spaces of my mind

All because of words that you strung together

And I decided then I wouldn't use my lips for harm

Even if they can't form anything else when it comes to you

You Were Made for an Epic

I could write a book on the pain I endured when I was with you. How you cut me open and filled me with your poison.

How the hate you felt for yourself grew on me like a fungus.

And I could write a song filled with lines of the sadness I've been left with. How you took the color out of my world and left me to live in the dark. Why my knuckles still ache from fighting off the demons you conjured here.

But I won't.

I don't want to waste the paper.

You aren't worth the ink.

And I know you think running away was the biggest favor you ever did for me, that you saved me from a lifetime of hurt.

And though you are partly right, you'll be back.

Because you're walking this earth in debt.

And not even someone like you can carry guilt like that around their neck forever.

It will demand your attention.

And while you're out there searching for me,

I'll be long gone.

You, Me, and Her

In a big city where men like you don't make it.

And women like me thrive.

I've got the scars to prove it.

I'll never let you find me,

Because that's your burden to carry.

You deserve it.

You'll spend years trying to convince yourself you're all paid up.

And I'll spend years scrubbing off your stench.

You linger here like rotten milk.

You'll wander the world collecting more tragedies.

And your history will soon weigh you down.

It'll show in the cracks on your face.

You'll never escape it.

And while you're out there, aimless

I'll be writing books filled with redemption and hope.

I'll write songs with lyrics of love and passion.

Because the only print you were ever meant for was a punch line.

And me,

tylyn taylor

I was made for an epic.

Wild Love

I am not always the best lover

Highly flawed is at the top of my resume

With self-deprecating as my first bullet point

I am horrible with money

Its value is not heavy with me

Or motivating to me

I hate planning

And I lose track of time always

You can't take me anywhere

My hair is always a mess

My clothes show the soft flesh of my torso

And I don't own a bra

I hate wearing shoes

Even in public places

I get drunk

And laugh really loud

But sing louder

I am not conventional

My feet are dirty

And I've got tattoos that cover up my fingers

The word "fuck" escapes from my mouth

More often than not

I am not the kind of girl you take home to your mom

Unless your mom likes to drink wine

And curses like a truck driver

But I am the kind of girl you connect with

The kind of lover who helps you find the world through a new lens

Who pulls you out of bed at 2am

To stand on the front porch and howl at the moon

And asks the stars to grant your wishes

You, Me, and Her

I'm the lover who encourages you to take risks

Who pulls your wildest dreams from your chest

And begs you to dance with them

Because I want to see you light up

The kind of lover who holds hands with your insecurities

Because they are a part of you

And I don't just want the pretty parts

I want the whole ugly beautiful mess

I'm the lover who tells you to jump

To run far

To go fast

I'm the lover who believes this life is short

And tragic

And fucking amazing

So if you're with me I want you to feel that

With your entire being

I am not the best lover

But that's okay

I am here to make you feel alive

To laugh and cry

And go crazy

So take my hand

And let's jump in.

Authentic

There is an overwhelming beauty in authenticity, even when that authenticity is paired with sorrow. To constantly radiate your true colors is to live consciously. Feeling everything all at once and letting those feelings dance in your eyes. To be unwavering in your truth, and unapologetic for that truth, is to live your life on purpose.

I met a friend's partner the other day. We talked story and laughed over wine and small plates. Nothing more, nothing less. We didn't dig deep into one another's histories or share tales of heartbreak. But when I excused myself to use the restroom he mentioned to my friend, his girlfriend, that he could tell I was broken. He could feel it.

And he was right.

I am broken. My energy emits it. My spirit is wired to convey the exact truth of its being. And right now, this is my truth. I am broken. I wear it like pearls around my neck. I am not ashamed. Because right now I can't untether myself from the veracity of my life as it stands in this moment. This is not to say that my energy lowers the frequency of those around me. On the contrary, I live my life to lift others up. My day is not over until I hear the laugher from someone else's throat.

My energy is not negative. I laugh, I smile, and I share. All of these things I do with fervor. All of these things are a part of me. But I don't just bring the pretty parts of myself to the table. I bring the ugly, the messy, the hard, and the delicate as well. And I ask those around me who take up my space to dance with them.

And I am not sorry if you don't want to climb through the rubbish with me. If it isn't your way of life, then we belong to different tribes. And that's okay. You see because I am glad that a stranger saw the entirety of my being the moment he met me.

That he was able to smile with me, and also see the cracks in my chest. Because our time here is short, and in the greater galaxy it is minute. But it is ours. So, we should spend it with people who grab the broken parts of us by the hand and say, "I've been there. I see you."

I am broken. But that doesn't mean I am unfixable. I will heal. I will emerge. And when I do my energy will carry it with me. That and everything else that I am and will be.

Extinguished Flame

I've seen hell in another man's eyes

The rage burning welts into my flesh

As I confronted the demon that lived in his chest

Begging it to inhabit me instead

Self-sacrificing in the name of attachment

But he would have killed me

If I kept trying to save him.

Makua

I swore I washed you off in the waves

But here you linger

Our bodies still printed in the sand

Where Makua watched me fall in love with you

And now this place feels a little less vibrant

Because she knows our secret

How we made love in her arms

And dishonored her by throwing each other away

I can ask her for the forgiveness

That you never begged me for

So I weep in her lap

Willing her to raise me up within her green body

And forgive me for taking a lover into her sacred home

One who didn't deserve to press his skin

On her holy land.

Monsters

Monsters don't hide under your bed

They fuck you and call it love making

They weave words like sticky webs that tangle you up

They don't wait in the dark

They slither next to you between the sheets

Gnawing at your neck

They whisper riddles into your ear that drive you mad

They fill you with their toxin

And laugh sinisterly as you slowly die

Monsters aren't imaginary

Monsters live right here.

Fighting Fear

I think so many of us are afraid of being alone that we miss out on a huge portion of the journey.

We let fear move through our veins as we try and navigate this life, all the while searching for something that we will never find if we don't learn to let go of the apprehension.

Because fear is just our innate ability to worry, after all, we are just humans.

But if you really take the time and energy to look within, you will see that our fears are based solely on something that hasn't even happened yet.

Finding the courage to know we must sit alone with ourselves to truly discover our complete authenticity is a gift. How can we discover what seeds are planted in our chests, what makes us feel alive, if we are always adapting to what those around us need us to be? What they want us to be?

Your authentic self will grow out of those seeds. And you will toil and sow the land and it will take work.

Like the earth, you will grow through the seasons. You will change. You will accept. You will bloom. And don't accept anything less than your true self.

Maybe this comes with a change of space, in a new city around different faces, urging you to see the world through fresh eyes.

Maybe it comes with a door closing, saying goodbye to people, places, and situations that you are no longer serving. Or that are no longer serving you.

This recognition comes with the promise of new beginnings. But we have to be fearless; we have to know that sometimes, the path is lonely.

So how do we combat this fear?

Be kind to yourself.

Hold yourself accountable.

Show up for yourself.

Make the time to work. Get in there and grind. Be raw.

This will lead to the version of yourself that you have always dreamed of.

And that version is the one you were meant to show this world. You deserve that. Those around you deserve that.

Take the time to dance with the fear. There is no way it burns brighter than the fire in your eyes, and the willingness to take on this journey.

You were made to tell a story. Let it be the one the galaxy wrote for you in the stars. The one begging you to find it in her cosmos.

You owe that much to yourself.

The Runner

She was always running

Exhausted pursuing the marvel

Hot on its tail

Wondering if she would ever catch it

Or if she'd be left unfulfilled

She longed for the ache in her chest to halt

For the blisters on her soles to heal

But she knew every crack

Every drop of blood

And hot heavy tear

Put her a pace ahead

So, she strides on.

Mixed Signals

It's not his fault

That I was writing his love story

While he was writing my tragedy.

Three's A Crowd

First there was her

And you broke her heart and threw it into the ocean

But came back for seconds

Just in case she had anything left in her chest

And you decided you didn't want just one lover

But as many as you could

Then there was me

And we overlapped

And you sang lies in my ear

I swore this was the big one

But you were still inside of her

When I told you I loved you

Now there's just you

And everything we shared is empty

Like your bed

I can't imagine living with a heart like yours

That devours people whole

tylyn taylor

And still ends up alone.

They Always Come Back

You aren't the first thing I think about when I wake up anymore

Or the last

And now that my wounds have healed

And the ache in my ribs have subsided

You show your face

And you want to hold my hand and revel in my glory

But where were you?

When I was deep in the trenches you dipped

Even when I begged you to pull me above the water

And I needed you

But you were scared

Now the promise of change fills your mouth

And you say you're sorry

But apologies can't change time

Or pay for my Xanax

I was under the impression you understood me better

tylyn taylor

That a goodbye with me is forever

And if you didn't want me at my lowest

There's no room for you up here.

Signs

I believe in signs

The moon doesn't just move the tides

She has a journey planned for each one

So don't question this moment

You are exactly where you are supposed to be

The universe will see you

Your adventure has been written in the stars

This experience is cosmically threaded for each one of us

So look around

Take this in

The people the atmosphere the time

All of it is here for you right now

And tomorrow may be different

People will come and go

Our space will change

But this is your journey

Don't waste your time trying to alter what is meant to be

tylyn taylor

Let it move you

The universe will step right in

When you need her to most

Until then let these moments fill you entirely.

Noise

I can't tell you how many times a man has commented on my body before he ever spoke about my mind. How many times I played into it, absorbing the compliments as if surface level observations could forge a deep connection between two souls. As if love could be built on comments about how great I look in that dress.

And I can't tell you how many times a man has looked right through me as I told him my wildest dreams. Only to snap back to reality when I was finished and ask me if I'd like to go home with him that night. My intellect having nothing to do with the nerves coursing through him. And I wonder if anyone of the opposite sex will ever want to hear my story before they undress me.

Because men have told me my entire life how I needed to be for them,

How I should sit still and look pretty.

Smile.

Don't be too loud.

But speak up when I need you to.

Don't wear that, it's too slutty.

You look like a prude.

I don't like your hair short.

Don't say that.

You're wrong.

You should wear more makeup.

And on and on it goes.

But I decided to change the game. Because baby this world is mine for the taking. And I didn't come here to fit your mold.

I came here to make noise.

And I don't give a fuck if my words turn you off.

Or if my skirt is too short.

If my opinion punches yours in the face.

I want to cause chaos for as long as I can. And I need you to challenge me.

Because you being able to unbutton my top quickly does nothing for me.

That move is played out.

Show me what lives in the corners of your mind. And hunt for what I keep hidden in my heart.

Let me see what you hide away in your rib cage.

Grab my hand and fling me into the unknown. Stand beside me and actually hear me. Memorize the color of my eyes before you make a map of my curves.

Because I'm sure you can make love to my body.

But can you handle a heart like mine? A mouth that spits fire, and a mind that creates magic. Because that's what I want. That's what turns me on. Let me see that you can handle a woman who fights to be everything she wants.

That you want to make noise with me.

That kind of chaos blows my mind.

So, rock my world, baby. I'm waiting.

Learning

Let this moment be a chapter

Not the entire book.

Mana

You are a wild thing

That grew in a garden of conformity

With fire inside of you

Aligned with the earth's core

One of Pele's daughters

Just waiting to erupt

Unpredictable

And Feral in your ways

They will try to tame you

To alter your truth

But it won't stick

Because you aren't meant for change

But for growth

In ways only the earth can fathom

Because you are made of the same molecules

So be relentless in your quest for expansion

You were not grown to be stationary

Be bold and fearless

These are the nutrients that feed you

And when the pursuit feels too heavy

Put your faith in her

She will carry you through.

Passion Fruit

I want to make your sheets sandy

My salty hair sticking to your neck

As you taste the mango juice

That drips from me when we touch

And your moan makes music in my ears

While my teeth connect with your flesh

And our bodies move with the waves

Under a moon that was meant for this moment.

Sunflower

I thought the first time I was with someone else

Would mean visions of your brown eyes watching me

And craving your touch on the small of my back

But it wasn't

It was nervous laughter

And the smell of tequila

It was beer pong in an empty bar

And rolled joints

Falling in like

Dancing in dark New York City alley ways

And his hands were stronger than yours

Without posing a threat

He called me beautiful

And I actually believed him

For the first time I finally felt safe

Lying next to long limbs that weren't my own

And he left me with a sunflower

You, Me, and Her

As he didn't occupy this space

And maybe our paths will never cross again

But that's okay

Because his touch taught me I don't have to live with you

Not here

Or anywhere ever again.

Finding Love

I hope this journey leads you to a place where you can love entirely.

And I don't just mean in the arms of the person who keeps your bones warm at night. But that you really feel it, stitched into the fabric of your soul.

That you find love within yourself during moments where you least expect it.

Like during solo movie dates, or dance parties in your bedroom, sipping red wine straight from the bottle.

And I hope loves energy pulses inside your veins, as you watch the sun rise in your favorite place.

Or smell a dish that you've been craving forever.

Love is the passion you pour out in words, and actions, wrapping itself around your heart.

Because we get so carried away in finding the magic that lives inside someone else's rib cage, we become blind to what has always radiated around us.

Love doesn't have to look tall dark and handsome.

Or like the girl across the hall.

Love can simply look like you.

And I hope to god you realize that you are all parts love. That you are not just another's half, or even their whole world.

Because you belong to you and you alone. And it isn't until we discover this, that we can truly share love on the same frequency with another.

So, find the love that has made home in your own heart, and spoil yourself with it.

Let it flow out of you.

Because love is so much more than the eyes of a partner.

Love is moving to the city you've always dreamed about.

Love is the wind that plays in your hair. In your laughter and smile.

Love is that first sip of coffee on a Sunday morning.

Love is everywhere, all around us.

Love is everything.

You, Me, and Her

This is for you,

The rebel woman with the loud voice. Who loves fiercely and fights like hell for what she believes in. The woman who ashes out cigarettes on the bottom of her combat boots, and marches in front of capital buildings.

For the woman who refuses to be silenced, who risks it all so her sisters have a voice.

Who wears dark eye makeup and has an envious collection of books.

For the warrior woman, who survives on black coffee, and curses like a truck driver.

Who doesn't give a fuck if her opinion turns you off, or her short skirt.

Because she's tough enough to let your judgments roll of her middle finger,

But still soft enough to love the entire world.

For the tough broads,

You are me.

This is for me,

The dreamer with her head constantly in the clouds. Who sees her future written in the stars.

You, Me, and Her

The gypsy woman who wanders the earth, planting love like wildflowers.

Who finds purpose in other people's laughter and imagines a world full of light.

The goddess with the soul that shifts like the tide with the moons pull and writes love letters to the sun.

The spiritual woman who doesn't rush to give herself to one person, because she finds meaning and life within herself.

Who shakes sand out of her hair, and lounges on sofas topless.

For the woman who has scrapes on her knees and elbows, because she falls down nine times and gets up ten.

Who lights fire in your soul and tucks your hair behind your ear.

Who finds home in every place she lands.

For the wild ones,

I am her.

This is for her,

For the woman who hasn't found her voice yet, who has put up with bullshit her whole life.

Who carries the weight of the entire world in her ribcage.

The woman whose womb has been home to others, and who's heart beats for them.

For the woman who works two jobs to just barely make it, who gives more of herself to others, than she has ever given to herself.

To the woman with skin color different than those around her every day, who speaks in melodies, but keeps quiet when their whispers sting her ears.

The woman whose love holds no identity but is ridiculed for the rainbow she pins to her jacket.

The woman who fills notebooks with ideas and creations but tucks it away under her bed each night.

For the woman who chases after him, who fears being alone.

To the silenced woman, who has yet to find the power that lives in her own throat.

For the ones ready to rise up,

You are me, and I am her, and she is you.

May we create a world where we are all seen. Where we are all heard. Where we all get a fighting chance.

This is for us.

Female

A beautiful woman can raise your vibrations

But a strong woman will increase your frequency.

This is for those who never stopped believing in me, even in my lowest moments. The souls who wrapped me up and reminded me that "I can." To anyone I have crossed paths with either in real time or virtually—your support and love mean everything to me, and I see you. For the men in my life who are beautiful examples of how brothers, partners, husbands, and fathers should be, I love you. And for all of the women in my life now, and in the future—you are strength. You are courage. You are light. I am inspired everyday by the grace and bravery I encounter from women. May we continue leading by example.

Acknowledgments

Mom, thank you for your constant love. For your humor in hectic situations. I love that you say the word 'fuck' now because you're "too old to care." You are the constant, and without you I am nowhere. To say you have sacrificed is the ultimate understatement. You are my best friend, my 16-year-old self's mortal enemy, my favorite person to impersonate, my strength, and my heart. Remember when I was a kid and never wanted to leave your side? I still feel that way. I love you.

Shelby and Alexis, thank you for being the women in my life. For loving me unconditionally, even when I make it really, really hard. Thank you for keeping me in check, and being as stubborn as I am. Bebe, you embody compassion and care. I've learned so much from you. Allie girl, you are everything good and sweet in this world and you carry it in your eyes. You are never alone. I will choose you both time and time again.

My Pukka fam, you made me laugh when I didn't think I could. You reminded me that there is beauty in simplicity, and you will forever hold a special place in my heart. Thank you.

Nicole, thank you for constantly reading, editing, crying, laughing, and doing all the things with me as we grow through these stages of life. We've done it all and have a thousand things left to experience. I love you.

Jason and Adam, thank you for being an example of good, kind, decent men. Thank you for loving me. I have admired you both since the moment I became your sister. I love you.

Lauren, my girlfriend, thank you for being a little ball of fire. For saving me countless times. Thank you for never giving up on me, no matter the distance or time. You've been the best kind of friend to me. Words can't express the gratitude I have for you.

My Hawaii fam, you helped me find myself. When I'm free, I'm with you. Thank you for your salty, beautiful love. I will never have a summer like the one I shared with you.

Melissa, thank you for believing in me before you even knew me. Your talent only rivals your beauty and strength as a woman. I feel so lucky to know you. Thank you for wanting to be a part of this and thank you for your beautiful work.

Conor, my instant family. The universe brought us together and now you're stuck with me forever. Thank you for making me laugh, and for believing in me and my crazy dreams. This book came together because of you helping me over wine on the hardwood floor. There is not another soul like you and I'm grateful to share in your journey. Thank you, I love you.

Dad, any words I could say would never compare to what you mean to me. My entire life you never once doubted that I could be anything and everything I wanted to be. Thank you for teaching me what it means to dream. These pages aren't here without your sacrifice. You are my hero, my favorite person, and the first phone call I make when anything happens. I made you a promise a long time ago that I would work my ass off to give you back everything you've ever given me. This is the start of that. I love you.

Norma Jane, the toughest woman I know. Thank you for raising me. Thank you for showing me that a stubborn woman is lethal and necessary. You have given all of us a family, a home in your arms, and laughter that fills our memories. There won't ever be another like you. I love you more than "tunken tell."

My Aunties, strong doesn't begin to explain what you all are. Unique in your own way, I have learned so much being your niece. Thank you for guiding me, taking care of me, and loving me through this life.

Yugen tribe, connection is deeper than exchanging words every day or seeing each other in close spaces. We may be spread across this country, but I hold you both in my heart everywhere I go.

Allyssa, thank you for seeing me in moments where I didn't recognize myself. Thank you for teaching

me that love doesn't look any certain type of way, and thank you for loving me.

Ili girl, thank you for holding me up when I'm weak. Thank you for forgiving me. For loving me. And being a part of my tribe. I love you forever.

Lucy girl, without you this book is still hiding in my journal. I don't think there are words that can truly express how you have changed my life. You are one of the most creative, intelligent, fun, and beautiful people I have come to know. Thank you for taking one look at me and knowing we were craigslist soul mates. You are my sister, my best friend, and an inspiration to me every day. Thank you for all of the work you have done for this project and for believing in something bigger. I can't wait to take over this city with you. I love you.

Gracie and Avery, you will never understand how much I love you. I can't wait to watch you grow into strong, sassy, beautiful young women. Being your auntie is my favorite thing in this world.

Haileigh Louise, the love of my life, this is for you. Thank you for teaching me what it means to love unconditionally. You are the kind of light this world needs. My wish is that you continue to grow up in a world that gives you wings and applauds you for being unapologetically yourself. I am nuts and crazy about you. You will never be alone in this world. I love you more and more every day. I can't wait to watch you be great.

And to you. Thank you for showing me I am strong on my own. Thank you for teaching me I can be completely selfless. You showed me what it meant to fall in love, and because of that I am grateful. I forgave you a long time ago, because forgiveness meant healing. And it was time to heal. I didn't create this in spite of you, I created this for me. To prove to myself that I am worthy. I am brave. And I am a fucking lady. And no one can take that away from me.

www.ingramcontent.com/pod-product-compliance
Lightning Source LLC
Chambersburg PA
CBHW022122040426
42450CB00006B/809